I'm Luke.
I don't like homework.
I fidget a lot.
I ask a lot of questions.
I jump, sing and act things out.
I imagine, draw and make things.
I remember by playing with words.

I learn by **doing**.

ISBN: 172509567X
ISBN-13: 978-1725095670

Very clever.

I knew you'd find a way to learn the months.

I'd find... WHAT?

Well, it's what you said when you ran into the house,

"Just for me a massive jumbo jet actually spiralled over nervous dads."

The first letter in each word is the first letter of each month, isn't it?

Just	**J**anuary
for	**F**ebruary
me	**M**arch
a	**A**pril
massive	**M**ay
jumbo	**J**une
jet	**J**uly
actually	**A**ugust
spiralled	**S**eptember
over	**O**ctober
nervous	**N**ovember
dads	**D**ecember

Mr Pug's
Special List of Silly Voices

I've just won a lottery! voice
I have a sore throat voice
I'm cute as a button voice
I'm a TV newsreader voice
I've just seen a ghost! voice
We are going to Disneyland! voice
I'm the Queen of England voice
I'm very very tired voice
I'm a giant (and I want to eat you) voice
I'm in a great hurry voice
I'm Father Christmas voice
I've just woken up voice
I'm freezing cold voice
I'm a shouty man voice
I'm on a rollercoaster voice
I'm eating with my mouth full voice
I've got my lips sealed voice
I'm a farm animal voice
I'm a tiny fairy voice
I'm only two years old voice
I'm an evil character voice
I'm a secret spy voice
I'm worried about this voice
I'm about to sneeze voice
I'm a policeman voice

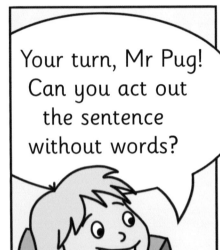

Your turn, Mr Pug! Can you act out the sentence without words?

Just for me

a massive

jumbo jet

actually

spiralled

over

nervous

dads

12

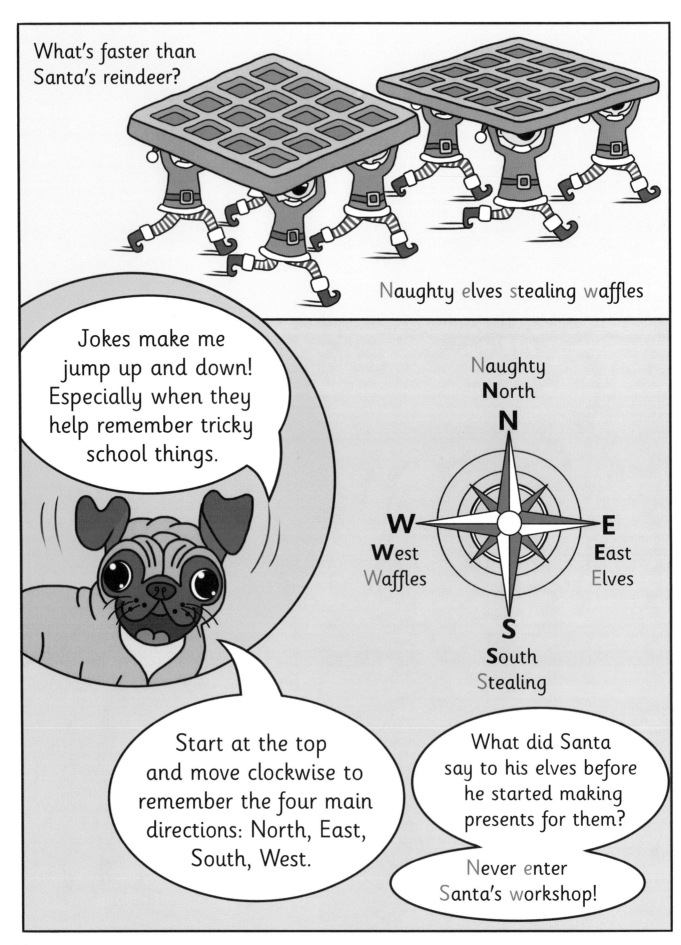

Go South,
then West.
Now East,
then North.

A zigzag!

North to South,
then East to West.

Nearly.
Was that West?

Knees up
and land on North.
Perfect!
Okay, now you're
showing off.

Spin around
and land on South.

You've learned
your directions
in no time!

Did you know?

- Learning by repeating things over and over, even writing them out many times, **doesn't work for everyone**.
- You might learn a new thing quicker if you **do something with it**.
- Doing funny, or even silly, things might help you learn quicker.
- Move your body when you're learning, and your brain will create extra memory networks – that way you'll remember the hard stuff for longer.

This part is best read with an adult, or you can read it to me instead.

- Funny and silly ways to make your brain remember hard stuff are called **mnemonics** [ne'monics]. Or you can call them **memory tricks**. They can be songs, rhymes, acronyms (LOL and NASA are examples), pictures, or phrases to help remember lists of things in an order.
- We remember **our own** memory tricks better than those given to us by other people. See if you can come up with your own sentences to remember the order of the months and the four main directions.

Things you can try out

- Share your memory tricks with others so they can remind you when you forget them.
- *Or* start a notebook to collect your very own fun memory tricks.
- Turn your memory tricks into pictures and posters, which you can display around the house, for example stick them on the fridge or your bedroom walls.
- Make a funny comic book about the thing that is hard to learn. Watch people laugh when you give it to them to read.
- Do a show about the tricky thing for your family or friends. Pretend shows for your pets, teddy bears or Power Rangers work just as well!
- Teach your family and friends, then quiz them for a super reward, for example an extra cuddly cuddle with you, or a picture/comic book made by you.
- Read to your pet or favourite toy. Teach them what you've learned. They secretly *love* it!
- Keep your hands busy when your brain is thinking hard. This will help you concentrate. When you're losing interest, grab a fidget or small fiddly construction toy. Busy hands mean calmer brain. Ahhh... Now I can think!

Monkeys	Monday
take	Tuesday
whatever	Wednesday
they	Thursday
find	Friday

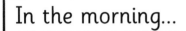

In the morning...

Hopscotch! Watch me.

noodles served us just mug very empty my

You said that last night.

First letter of each word... Remember?

I'm out of breath now. Your turn.

My	Mercury
very	Venus
empty	Earth
mug	Mars
just	Jupiter
served	Saturn
us	Uranus
noodles	Neptune

What to do when you're *really* stuck

- If something looks impossible at first, break it into parts and start with the easiest bit.
- Don't blame yourself if something is hard. Maybe you haven't tried what works for your brain best yet.
- Ask for help (because that thing won't go away). Look at the messages below. Ask an adult to photocopy them for you, or make your own, so you can give (one or two at a time) to the adult who is ready to help.

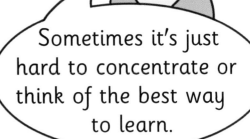

Sometimes it's just hard to concentrate or think of the best way to learn.

This is hard for me. Could we turn it into play, please?

This homework takes a long time. I need a cuddle and a joke.

Let's have a think about how I could learn this in a different way.

I learn by acting things out. Ready for my amazing performance?

Could we learn this in the garden/park? I learn better when I'm 'on the go'.

I'm itching for a fidget or fiddling toy. It helps me focus.

Let's make silly stories and songs about this so I won't forget.

Could we learn this bit in the kitchen, the other bit in the lounge, and the last bit in my bedroom?

Could we try 5 minutes play, then 10 minutes of homework, and so on...

Let's go outside and learn with chalk, sticks and pebbles before I write in my book.

Once you've played with them, you remember the hardest of spellings.

Magic?? I really need to tell you about...

Nooo way!!

Yes way. I can now spell 'porridge'

Porridge?

My pet's name.

Can we use the letters to learn spellings for school?

Yes, but it'll be our secret, okay?

Pinky promise!

Did you know?

- 'Look, cover, write, check' **doesn't work for everyone**.
- Your brain will remember the letters' order quicker if you let it *discover* it for itself. It'll enjoy feeling the letters and linking them together.
- When we look down on paper and see the word already spelled for us, the brain doesn't feel there's much for it to do. When you *recognise* the word, it doesn't mean you actually *remember* the letters' order.

I used to hate spelling. Now it's my favourite homework.

- When we close our eyes to feel the letters on the table, it's very easy to lose balance and fall off the chair! Always make sure your feet are firmly on the floor, or are resting on the chair bars. I know a boy who likes to have cushions around his chair when learning to spell. Just in case!
- It's best to do the letter feeling activities when someone is with you to guide your fingers and check the word is spelled correctly. Imagine learning the wrong spelling!
- Learning to spell is quicker when you look for small words within words (for example 'tom-or-row') or letter patterns (for example 'eve' has a 'v' sandwiched between two letters 'e').

Things you can try out

- Ask an adult to look for wooden letters online, and whether they can afford them. Low-cost wooden letters will work just as well as more expensive ones.
- *Or* you can ask the adult to help you cut out letters out of cardboard. Printable lower case letter templates can be found online.
- *Or* you can use alphabet pasta or alphabet cereal instead.
- Why not personalise your letters with different colours, patterns and pictures on them? It'll make you *love* your letters even more.
- If you know the alphabet, always start spelling activities by arranging all your letters in front of you in an alphabetical order. If you don't know the alphabet yet, ask the adult to do this for you.
- If you don't like closing your eyes for longer than a moment, feel the letters under a towel or cushion instead.
- Come up with your own letter feeling games and share your ideas with others.

Wait... What goes after 'qu'...

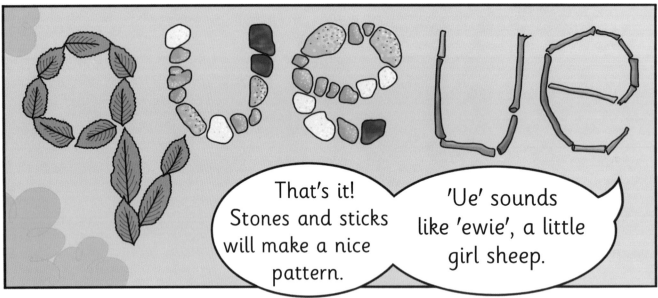

That's it! Stones and sticks will make a nice pattern.

'Ue' sounds like 'ewie', a little girl sheep.

And is so easy to draw in the air. It just glides along. Baa! Baa! Here comes another ewie.

61

How about finding your 'writing' paw? I write with my right hand, so I know where the right side is.

Will it work if I write with my left paw? The right one never felt right..., which explains... Gotcha, left 'writing' paw = left side.

Focus, Mr Pug. I touch my left whisker with my right paw.

BOOM!

See, it's easy now. You can do this, Mr Pug!

SMASH!

BANG!

CRASH!

Now, that's what I call getting magic to work!

Outta here!

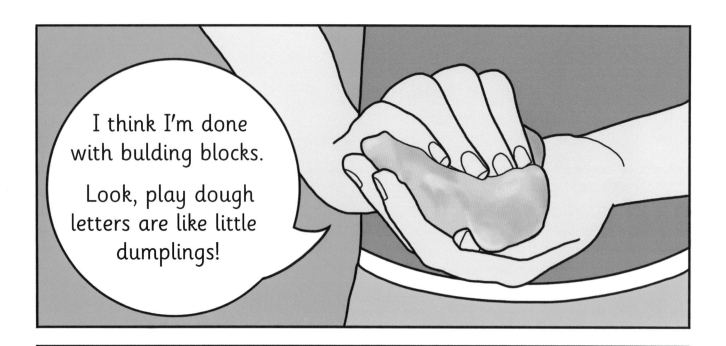

I think I'm done with bulding blocks.

Look, play dough letters are like little dumplings!

I love them! I think we've done really well, Sophie.

Why don't we leave our work here and check if the letters have been returned. We have been clever!

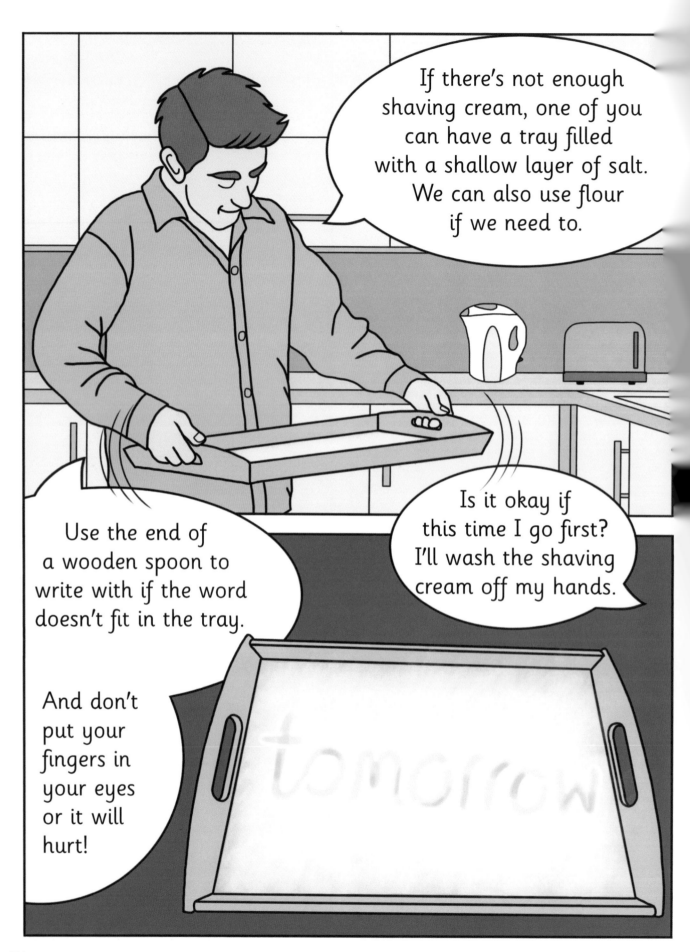

It doesn't add up

Why?

Mr Pug is on our team

So?

He wouldn't lie to us

But he likes games

Did you know?

🐾 Learning doesn't have to be boring. You can learn in lots of FUN ways.

🐾 Play is one of the best ways to learn.

🐾 The learning strategy based on play is called **multisensory** because it allows you to use different senses all at the same time: seeing, hearing, touching, feeling, smelling, tasting, and being aware of things in time and space.

Have you seen a pug copy spellings on paper? Me neither. Just saying...

🐾 **Multisensory learning** helps us concentrate better, even on things that we normally find hard to focus on, for example spellings. That's why when you play with fidgets and small construction toys, you realise that you can listen and understand without being confused.

🐾 **Emotions** also help us learn: excitement, happiness, pride, wonder, surprise, trust, slight anxiety. Your brain is at its sharpest when you're waiting for something exciting to happen, waiting to find out something that is puzzling you, or revving to show that you can do something well.

🐾 Playing adventure games ties multisensory experience and positive emotions together.

Things you can try out

🐾 Have Luke and Sophie inspired you to start your own spelling adventure? Plan yours today. Make sure it's safe and the adults know where you are and what you're doing.

🐾 Use multisensory objects to learn anything hard, not only spellings. Use building blocks, kitchen pots and jugs, small counters and string to understand tricky parts of maths.

🐾 Ask an adult to help you make your own paper plate clock to learn to tell the time. Attach the short hand to the clock to tell hours before adding the long hand to learn minutes. Learn about quarters using building blocks. It'll all make sense when you look at the clock. Or help the adult bake a small pie and eat it quarter by quarter.

🐾 Tell your teacher how you've learned something hard so they can plan similar activities at school.

🐾 Make a picture or comic book about your way of learning tricky school things. Share it with others so they can learn, and enjoy it, too.

🐾 Whatever you do, have FUN, or come back to learning after you've had a little rest.

What **REALLY** happened...

Your Turn

to go on an adventure.
Have fun
learning by doing!